I am delighted to introduce this excellent book and to have an opportunity to thank all you people who have made Hägar so popular. In 1972, my father, Dik Browne, created an overweight, ill-mannered and misunderstood Viking chieftan named 'Hägar the Horrible'. The comic strip was to become his job, hobby, confessional and a kind of autobiography in pictures. Like Hägar's son, Hamlet, I seemed destined to follow in my father's footsteps. I became apprenticed to my dad in 1972, writing gags and fetching coffee. He taught me everything I know about cartooning. Now when I draw cartoons, I also draw on everything dad taught me. Working on his strip keeps me in touch with his spirit. I'm reminded all the time of his wit, charm, strength, good deeds and great kindness. But enough of this! There are worlds to conquer! Dragons to slay! Knights to battle and maidens to save! Welcome to the world of Hägar the Horrible.

Chris Browne.

Contents

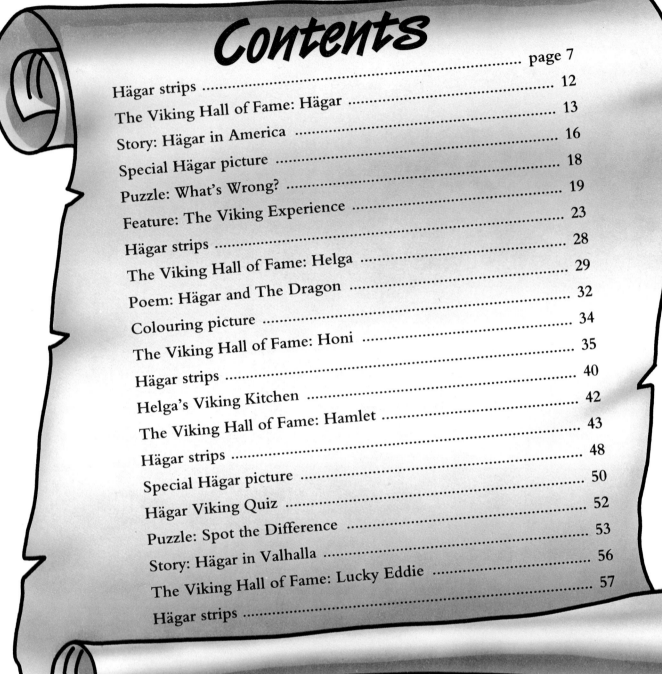

.... page 7

Hägar strips 12

The Viking Hall of Fame: Hägar 13

Story: Hägar in America 16

Special Hägar picture 18

Puzzle: What's Wrong? 19

Feature: The Viking Experience 23

Hägar strips 28

The Viking Hall of Fame: Helga 29

Poem: Hägar and The Dragon 32

Colouring picture 34

The Viking Hall of Fame: Honi 35

Hägar strips 40

Helga's Viking Kitchen 42

The Viking Hall of Fame: Hamlet 43

Hägar strips 48

Special Hägar picture 50

Hägar Viking Quiz 52

Puzzle: Spot the Difference 53

Story: Hägar in Valhalla 56

The Viking Hall of Fame: Lucky Eddie 57

Hägar strips ....

Copyright © 1991 King Features Syndicate, Inc.

Published by Ravette Books Limited 1991

Printed and bound for Ravette Books Limited,
3 Glenside Estate, Star Road, Partridge Green,
Horsham, West Sussex RH13 8RA by
Proost International Bookproduction

ISBN: 1 85304 279 X

HÄGAR IN AMERICA

"I d-d-don't feel very well!" groaned Hägar, clinging to the mast of his longboat as it pitched and tossed in a fierce Atlantic storm. "Neither do I!" wailed Lucky Eddie, who was hiding under the ship's cargo in mortal terror. "I want my money!" "You mean your 'Mummy'," corrected Hägar. "Do you have to get everything wrong?" "I want my *money!*" insisted Eddie. "For this voyage. Then I can spend it before it's too late!" "Give me strength!" sighed Hägar.

The sky grew darker by the minute and thunder and lightning were added to the noise of the raging sea. Huge waves towered over the little longboat, making it rise and fall like a seagull riding the air-currents. "Let's pretend we're at the funfair!" cried Hägar, trying to be brave. "This is the best roller-coaster ride we've ever had!" "No, it isn't!" muttered Lucky Eddie. "No, it isn't!" agreed Hägar.

Suddenly, there was a deafening CRACK! "The mast has snapped," gasped Hägar, looking horrified, "and what's worse – it's hit Lucky Eddie on the head." The fat Viking lurched over to his hapless companion who lay spread-eagled on the deck. "Are you okay, Ed?" exclaimed Hägar, anxiously. "It would appear I've escaped this unfortunate mishap!" said Eddie. "EH?" gulped Hägar. "My cranium's intact, I'm pleased to report. Now let's see – what's the best way to get out of this situation . . ?"

Hägar took two steps backwards and fell over the cargo. He sat up and blinked at Eddie in amazement. "That blow on the head seems to have changed his personality!" thought Hägar. "He's brainy now!" "My advice would be," continued Lucky Eddie, "to abandon ourselves to the wind and the tide. With no mast, we are at the mercy of the sea. Let it carry us where it will!" Hägar felt in no position to argue, so he nodded his head in agreement. "A storm I can cope with," he muttered, "but a *brainstorm* is quite a different matter!"

Hägar closed his eyes and left himself to his fate. He must have dropped off to sleep because, some time later, there was a sharp jolt and he found himself pitched head-first out of the boat! It was a soft landing and, scrambling to his feet, Hägar realised what was under his feet. "Sand!" he yelled, throwing his arms up in the air in delight. "We've made it home!" "I think your jubilation is a little premature!" commented Eddie. "What?" said Hägar.

Lucky Eddie indicated the scene in front of them – a huge, rolling plain which stretched away into the distance, as far as the eye could see. "Not Norway?" gulped Hägar. Lucky Eddie shook his head. "Not Sweden . . . or Denmark . . . or England . . . or France . . . or any other place I've visited and sacked?" Eddie shook his head again. "Where, then?" asked Hägar. "A vast new land on the other side of the Atlantic Ocean," explained Eddie. "I once heard Erik the Red talking about it on a Chat Show." Hägar was not excited by this news. "I hate visiting new lands," he muttered, "there's a chronic shortage of bars and restaurants."

Hägar looked round for some wood to repair their damaged longboat, but Eddie would not help him. "I don't think we should go home," he said, a strange visionary light shining in his eyes. "I think we should stay here. This is a land of infinite possibilities." "What are you talking about now?" grumbled Hägar, watching his friend wandering around as if in a trance. "This will be a rich land in the future!" exclaimed Eddie, flinging out one arm. "I see wheat, cattle, hamburgers, apple pie . . . and a wonderful drink made from cola beans!" "Is it alcoholic?" asked Hägar, eagerly, "No!" replied Eddie. "Then we don't want it!" snapped Hagar. "Come and help me fix the boat!"

The days passed and, eventually, the repairs were complete. But still Lucky Eddie did not want to leave. "Is there nothing that will persuade you to come home?" cried Hägar. "Nothing!" replied Eddie, firmly. Next moment, there was a loud TWANG and an arrow whizzed over Lucky Eddie's head and stuck in a nearby tree. Looking up, the two Vikings saw a hoarde of Red Indians, their faces bright with warpaint, bearing down upon them. "Quick! Into the boat!" yelled Hägar. "I don't think the locals want you to stay and make cola!"

Hägar and Eddie scrambled away in their longboat with a hail of arrows raining down around them. As the coast of their new-found-land disappeared over the horizon, Eddie felt a tear starting to run down his cheek. "Don't stand there blubbing," snapped Hägar, "grab hold of the rudder and steer the boat. And keep your head out of the way of the sail. I haven't fixed the boom very well and it's liable to swing round and hit you." "Don't you start bossing me about again . . ." began Eddie. Then, ZONK! The boom swung round and hit Eddie on the head!

Poor Eddie lay senseless in the bottom of the boat all the way back to Norway. Helga's tender loving care could not revive him; nor could Dr Zook's medicinal potions. It was not until Hägar took off his socks (well, he *had* been wearing them for nearly six months) that Eddie was startled back into consciousness. "Where am I?" he spluttered. "Home!" replied Hägar. "No, I'm not!" retorted Eddie. "This is *your* home – not *my* home!" "Things are looking up!" thought Hägar.

When Hägar was sure that Eddie was steady on his feet, the two friends walked back to Eddie's house. 'I'll check out my theory as we go," thought Hägar. "Tell me, Eddie," he said, casually, "what's a myth?" "That's easy," smiled Eddie, "it's a little fluttery thing, like a butterfly." "And a magnet?" added Hägar. "Er . . . that's a horrible little worm," replied Eddie, "you find them in apples." "Now tell me," concluded Hägar, "which is your right hand and which is your left?" "Do you think I'm stupid or something?" snorted Eddie, holding up his hands. "This is my right and this is my left. No, wait a minute. Maybe it's the other way round! Let me think – people write with their right hands . . . unless they're left-handed. That's right. I mean – that's left. Oh, dear! I'm pointing in two different directions at once now!" Hägar put his arm round his friend's shoulder. "Nice to have you back, Lucky Eddie!" he grinned.

From that day on, Eddie never mentioned the land beyond the ocean. Hägar did not mention it, either. "I'm happy with the *Viking* dream," he chuckled, "sacking, looting and pillaging!"

What's Wrong?

Here are four pictures of Hägar and his family. Each picture has a deliberate mistake in it. Can you see what's wrong?

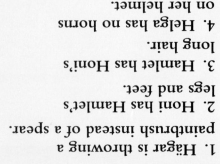

18

The Viking Experience

The Jorvik Viking Centre in York is a museum with a difference. Instead of the usual array of exhibits in glass cases, modern technology has been used to *recreate* the past and bring history to life. You travel in a Time Car which takes you back through 1000 years of British history before stopping in the Viking Age. Here, the sights, sounds and smells of Viking York have been reconstructed with immense care from the evidence of archaeology. As you travel through the teeming market-place, you are HERE and you are THERE – both at the same time! It's a real experience of the Vikings!

For all you Hägar fans who have not yet visited the Jorvik Centre (or to remind those of you who have), here is a sample of some of the scenes on view . . .

LOTHIN'S WOOD STALL

SVEIN'S LEATHER SHOP

SNARRI THE JEWELLER

THE COOPERS OF COPPERGATE

A Viking Home

Inside ▲

Outside ▼

21

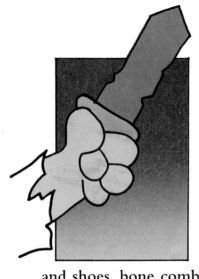

The Dig

The Jorvik Viking Centre was made possible by an archaeological dig that took place in York between 1976 and 1981. In an area of the city known as Coppergate, the remains of Viking York were found buried deep below the modern streets. It was an exciting find because the damp soil had preserved the timber buildings and objects inside them. Whole streets of houses, shops, workshops and warehouses were discovered, as well as 30,000 everyday objects including Viking cutlery, keys, brooches, boots and shoes, bone combs and storage jars. But instead of confining this rich haul to cupboards and catalogues, and the knowledge gained to history books, the York Archaeological Trust took the bold step of using their find to tell the story of Viking York. So they built the Jorvik Viking Centre in the huge hole created by the dig!

It has proved a successful move. The imaginative concept of the museum won the 1987 National Marketing Award and has ensured a constant stream of visitors, all eager to take part in 'the Viking experience'.

The dig itself has also been recreated using life-size model figures

Some of the Viking objects found at Coppergate

Photographs and information kindly supplied by the Jorvik Viking Centre.

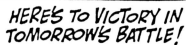

SOUNDS LIKE DADDY GOT UP ON THE WRONG SIDE OF BED

12-13

READY?

READY!

SOMEDAY, THEY'LL PROBABLY HAVE AN EASIER WAY TO GET TO THE TOP

12-14

I TRY TO SAVE MONEY BUT, EVERY TIME I DO, YOU BUY A NEW BOAT!

DON'T WORRY, BABY— SOME DAY OUR SHIP WILL COME IN

WHAT SHIP ?!!

DIK BROWNE 12-16

I HATE TO SEE A LOOSE STRAW HANGING DOWN FROM MY ROOF

WHUMP!

≳SIGH≲

DIK BROWNE 12-17

Hägar and The Dragon
A Viking Saga

I tell my tale of ancient days,
When the land was filled with woes,
And life was spent in fear and dread
Of the dragon, Smokeynose.

'Twas on that fateful Tuesday,
When Hägar hurried home,
"These flowers are for your birthday.
I brought them back from Rome!"

Helga looked at Honi,
Behind her on the stool,
"Those flowers are from the garden!
The man thinks I'm a fool!"

Then Helga's face turned red with rage,
"Each year's just the same!
Your present is an insult –
It's driving me insane!
Well, this year will be different,
I want a decent gift,
A golden necklace, brooches, jewels!"
"Oh, dear!" thought Hägar, miffed.

Hägar ran to Eddie,
His friend through thin and thick,
"I need to find some treasure –
And I need to find it quick!"
Eddie's face went white with fear,
"B-B-But everybody knows,
All the treasure in this land
is kept by Smokeynose!"

Hägar rushes to find his sword,
"No dragon frightens me!
If Helga doesn't get a prezzie
I don't get my tea!"

Hägar went to a lonely cave,
High up in the hills,
And his eyes lit up with joy and glee,
"Now I can pay my bills!"
For, lying on the damp cave floor,
Was treasure in a sack,
Hägar nipped inside and grabbed it,
"Right, Eddie, let's get back!"

They had not gone hundred steps,
(Or maybe fifty more),
When the air was rent by
    a fearsome sound –
A dragon's angry roar!

Looking round, they saw a sight
Which gave them quaking knees,
Smokeynose in hot pursuit!
"Quick, Eddie – up this tree!"

Our two heroes sat and shook
As the dragon puffed and snorted,
Said Eddie: "I think this mission
Should really be aborted!"

"Never!" cried Hägar, feeling brave,
"This dragon's breath makes me sick,
But I've been eating curry,
Radishes and garlic!"
So Hägar breathed back at the beast
Whose fiery breath abated,
Then there came a mighty THUD –
Smokeynose had fainted!

"Quick!" cried Hägar. "Let's be gone!
I think we've won the battle.
I'll give Helga all these trinkets,
That'll stop her cackle!"

But news of Hägar's victory
Soon spread far and wide.
People flocked to see him
And gathered at his side.

"You owe me quids," said Doctor Zook,
"Me, too," said Lawyer Koyer,
Then the Tax Man Hurried o'er,
"How lucky that I saw ya!"
By the time they all were happy,
Hägar's loot had vanished!
"It isn't fair!" the Viking sobbed,
"I shall still be banished!"

So Hägar picked more flowers,
From Eddie's house this time,
But Helga would have none of it,
"I'm not falling for that line!

You promised me a necklace,
Or something made of gold,
They say you caught a wonderous beast –
You couldn't catch a cold!"

But Hägar became a hero,
For Smokeynose ceased to roar,
And without this treasure-trove to guard,
He took a job abroad.

So Hägar was forgiven,
And the world was filled with glee,
Until, a few weeks later,
He forgot his anniversary!

Then Helga blushed with rage again,
And blasted Hägar's ear,
Sighed Hägar: Smokeynose has gone –
But there's still a dragon here!

And the moral of this saga is:
'HELL HATH NO FURY
LIKE A WOMAN HORNED'

CO
P

You can co
returning h
paints

LOOK! THE CHRISTMAS STAR!

MAKE A WISH FOR SOMETHING YOU REALLY WANT!

WHAT I HOPE TO GET FOR CHRISTMAS IS A NEW SWORD, A FISHING ROD AND A KEG OF ENGLISH ALE

WHAT DO **YOU** WANT FOR CHRISTMAS, HAMLET?

PROMISE YOU WON'T LAUGH, DAD?

OF COURSE

OKAY—I WANT PEACE ON EARTH AND NO MORE WARS

THAT'S A LOVELY GIFT! **I'D** LIKE AN END TO HUNGER EVERYWHERE

AND **I'D** LIKE TO SEE MORE LOVE IN THE WORLD!

MAYBE IF ENOUGH PEOPLE ASK FOR THOSE THINGS FOR CHRISTMAS THEY MIGHT HAPPEN

UH... IS IT TOO LATE FOR ME TO CHANGE MY SELECTIONS?

12-25

DIK BROWNE

38

Helga's Viking Kitchen

When Hägar returns home from a hard day's looting and pillaging, there's nothing he likes better than to sit down and tuck into some traditional Viking fare. Sometimes, of course, Helga gives Hägar warmed-up left-overs, but if she's in a good mood (when Hägar's done some jobs round the house, for example, or given her something from his travels – like Greenland), she serves him his favourite Viking snack – oatcakes washed down with honey-wine (mead).

Both items on this menu are easy to make and, being a generous woman, Helga has decided to share her age-old recipes with the Great British Public. If however, you decide to have a go at making oatcakes or mead, remember to ask a grown-up if it's all right to use the kitchen or have one with you when you are cooking.

Traditional Oatcakes

You will need:

4oz (100g) flour	2oz (50g) butter	½ teaspoon bicarbonate of soda
4oz (100g) rolled oats	1oz (25g) lard	1 tablespoon water
1oz (25g) caster sugar	A pinch of salt	A little milk

Method:

1. Sieve the flour into a bowl and add the rolled oats, sugar and salt.

2. Take a small saucepan and melt the butter, lard, bicarbonate of soda and water.

3. Add this mixture to the dry ingredients and beat well. Then add enough milk to make a firm dough.

4. Roll out the dough to a thickness of about ¼ inch (5mm). Cut out into small circles, using a pastry cutter.

5. Place, well spaced out, on a greased baking tray and bake for about 15 minutes at 375F/190°C until pale golden brown.

6. Cool and serve on their own or with soft cheese.

(Makes about 25)

MEAD ‹Non alcoholic›

You will need:

8 pints (4.5 litres) water

2lbs (900g) honey

1 pint (600ml) of non-alcoholic white wine

1oz (25g) yeast

The peel of 2 lemons

2 crushed whole nutmegs

Method:

1. Bring the water and honey to the boil. Remove any scum from the surface and simmer gently for about 1 hour.

2. Pour into an earthenware container and leave to cool until just hot enough to touch.

3. Add the yeast and leave it to work. When the mixture has stopped 'hissing', add the white wine and the lemon peel.

4. Hang the two crushed nutmegs in the liquid and leave for about a week. Then strain and pour into bottles. Do not put the tops on until the liquid has stopped bubbling.

5. Keep the mead for as long as you can before drinking it. The older it is, the better it tastes!

WHAT A LOVELY DAY TO START THE NEW YEAR!

HAPPY NEW YEAR

UP AND AT 'EM, HAGAR!

OH, GOOD! YOU'RE UP AND DRESSED!

I HAVE A LOT OF THINGS FOR YOU TO DO TO START THE NEW YEAR RIGHT!

I WANT YOU TO PAINT THE KITCHEN WALLS... REPAIR THE CHIMNEY...

CLEAN OUT THE BARN... CHOP SOME WOOD...

BUILD A FENCE AND WASH THE FLOORS

WHAT DO YOU WANT TO DO FIRST?

DIK BROWNE 1-1

HÄGAR'S Viking Quiz

Here are 10 quiz questions to find out how much YOU know about Vikings and their world . . .

1 The Vikings were maurauding sailors and settlers who came from three different Scandinavian countries. Can you fill in the names of the countries?
N – – – – –. S – – – – –. D – – – – – –.

2 The Viking Age is said to begin with a raid on a famous monastery in Northumberland in 793. What is it called?
(a) Lindisfarne.   (b) Kells

3 What is the proper name for the deep-water bays and inlets from which the Vikings launched their longboats?

4 When two Viking ships wanted to communicate with one another, they used Norse Code.
(a) True?   (b) False?

5 What is the connection between the Vikings and Thursday, our fifth day of the week?

6 When an important Viking chieftan died, what usually happened to his body?
(a) It was buried.
(b) It was put in his longboat which was set on fire.
(c) It was preserved by enbalming.

7 Alfred the Great was the only Anglo-Saxon king who was strong enough to resist the invasion of the Vikings. Can you fill in the name given to the area in the North of England to which he confined them?
THE D — — — — — —.

8 Canute was a Viking warrior who became King of all England in 1017. For what famous action has he always been remembered?

9 Historians say that the Viking Age came to an end in 1066. Why?
(a) All the Vikings went home.
(b) The Vikings started to fight amongst themselves.
(c) The Normans led by William the Conqueror invaded from France.
(d) The Vikings lost all their ships in a terrible storm.

10 Magnus Magnusson, the presenter of BBC TV's 'Mastermind' quiz, is a well-known authority on the Vikings and a translator of Icelandic Viking sagas.
(a) True?   (b) False?

HAVE A NICE DAY!!

ANSWERS
1. NORWAY
   SWEDEN
   DENMARK
2. (a) Lindisfarne
3. Fjords
4. (b) False
5. Thursday is named after Thor, the Viking god of thunder ('Thor's day')
6. (b) It was put in his longboat which was set on fire.
7. The Danelaw
8. He commanded the sea to retreat (to demonstrate the power of kings)
9. (c) The Normans led by William the Conqueror invaded from France.
10. (a) True

spot the difference

There are 10 differences between these two pictures of Hägar in his favourite place – the pub! How many can you spot?

ANSWERS

From left to right, the following items are missing from picture 2:

1. Part of the window-lattice.
2. The shading on the back of the chair.
3. The knot in the wood at top of big pillar.
4. One of the bars of Hägar's stool.
5. The criss-cross on Hägar's leggings.
6. The handle of Hägar's beer-mug.
7. The top of the vase on the floor.
8. The pencil behind the barman's ear.
9. One of the cat's eyes.
10. The cork in the top of the bottle.

52

HÄGAR IN VALHALLA

CLANG! CLASH! The sound of battle echoed round the green French valley on a sunny morning in May. "What a way to earn a living!" thought Hägar, holding up his shield to ward off another blow from the furious Norman Knight. "It's hard work being a Viking hero!"

It had started out as a normal days' work. Hägar had sailed to Northern France, spotted a nice-looking Norman castle and got his men to smash the door down with a view to looting and plundering. The owner of the castle, a bad-tempered Frenchman called Le Duc de Pond, did not take kindly to this idea and came out to do battle in defence of his possessions. So Hägar found himself locked in mortal combat while his men looked on, cheering and eating biscuits like a crowd at a prize-fight.

All day long the noise of battle rolled, across the quiet meadows to the shimmering sea where Hägar's longboat lay waiting. By teatime, Hägar had had enough. "I've had enough!" he told the Duke. "It's teatime!" In response, the battle crazed Frenchman struck another stinging blow which Hägar just managed to parry with his trusty short-sword. "Have it your way," he sighed wearily, "I'll work overtime!" By nightfall, the two warriors were nearing exhaustion. "Listen, pal," groaned Hägar, "why don't we call it a day? I mean enough's enough and all that!" To his surprise, the Duke nodded his head and muttered, "Oui!" "Thank goodness for that!" exclaimed Hägar, putting down his sword and turning his back. "Come on, lads," he called, "home-time!"

It was a fatal mistake! Seeing his chance, the wicked Norman struck a further blow and Hägar fell to the ground. "Tell Helga I'll be late for supper . . ." he whispered, as darkness overtook him.

When Hägar awoke, he found himself sitting in a beautiful garden with trees and flowers all around and clear blue skies above. "Where am I?" muttered Hägar, as a pretty bird flew down and perched on his foot. "Valhalla!" replied the bird. "You're in Valhalla – home of all Viking heroes."

Hägar got up and looked around. "Nice bit of scenery," he commented, "if you like that sort of thing. Personally, I prefer the sight of a couple of roast oxen and six barrels of beer." "Later!" boomed a deep voice. "The feasting will be later!" Hägar jumped three feet in the air and landed in a dew-pond beside the path. "W-W-Who's there?" he stammered, looking round at the empty landscape. "Thor!" said the voice. "I am Thor!" "I'm thorry to hear that," replied Hägar, getting to his feet, "Have you just hit your head on something?" "THOR!" roared the voice. "The Viking god of Thunder." "Of course!" laughed Hägar. "I remember now."

Thor commanded Hägar to go to a golden hall he could see in the distance. "There, you will be reunited with other famous Vikings like Ragnar Hairy Breeches and Harald Bluetooth!" explained Thor, before departing in a peal of thunder. "I don't want to see *them* again!" muttered Hägar. "I owe them all money." However, the rumbling in Hägar's stomach was getting louder than Thor's thunder, so the fallen warrior stumbled to the hall in search of food and drink. He was not disappointed. Inside, he found a sumptuous spread equal to anything that Helga had produced for Christmas. "Attack!" whooped Hägar, charging to a wooden chair with his name carved in gold letters on the back.

CHOMP! SLURP! Hägar feasted until his stomach was so big that his trousers fell down – and then he feasted some more. It was not until he reached for his final juicy chicken drumstick that he realised the silence that had fallen all round him. "Wassamatter?" he mumbled, his mouth full of food. "Why aren't you singing and carousing like they do at Viking feasts?" "Your table-manners are disgusting!" exclaimed Ragnar Hairy Breeches. "And you need a bath!" added Harald Bluetooth. "You smell!" "But I'm a Viking!" protested Hagar. "What's that got to do with it?" snorted Ragnar. "If we've got to spend Eternity with you, you can at least be pleasant company." "More to the point," put in Harald, coming over and prodding Hägar on the chest with his stubby finger, "you owe us money. When are you going to pay up?"

Meanwhile, back home, the news of Hägar's tragic battle had just reached Helga. She stood on the seashore, looking at Hägar's longboat bobbing in the waves. "He loved that boat!" she sniffed, "and he loved me too, in his rough Viking way."

Gathering Honi under one arm and Hamlet under the other, Helga returned slowly to the house. "It's going to be strange not to see Daddy sitting in his chair!" sighed Honi. As they went in through the door, however, a familiar sound greeted their ears. Snoring! And a familiar figure sat slumped in the chair, fast asleep. "Dad's back!" cheered Hamlet.

Helga woke her husband up. "What happened, Hägar?" she cried. "I thought you were in Valhalla." "They didn't want me!" grinned Hägar. "They sent me back again!" "WE want you!" exclaimed Honi, rushing forward to cuddle her father. "Agreed!" laughed Hamlet and Helga, joining the embrace. When they had finished squeezing him, Hägar looked about three stone thinner and his trousers fell down again. "Which reminds me," smiled Hägar, "what's for supper? We ought to have a slap-up meal to celebrate my return."

When the table was set and Hägar had downed most of the contents, the Viking hero told of his adventures. "So," he concluded, "it's business as usual."

"You can say that again!" muttered Helga.

the viking hall of fame

lucky eddie

IT'S 20 MILES TO OSLO AS THE CROW FLIES

HOW FAR IS IT AS THE PEOPLE WALK?

HOLD IT!

UH-OH... NO WAY TO GET ACROSS

WE'LL HAVE TO BUILD A BRIDGE

WITH WHAT, KNUCKLEHEAD?!

DON'T CALL ME THAT! IT JUST SO HAPPENS I'VE GOT IT ALL FIGURED OUT!

O.K.! O.K.! I'M SORRY!

WE'LL USE THOSE TREES OVER THERE

DIK BROWNE 1-8

59

SVENSON WOULD LIKE TO HAVE A FEW WORDS WITH YOU, SIR

DON'T TELL ME HE WANTS TO TAKE ANOTHER SICK DAY!

YOU'VE GOT **STRESS**

GET OUT MORE! TRAVEL! MEET NEW PEOPLE!

THAT'S HOW I **GOT STRESS!**

HELGA, DO YOU THINK I COULD... **NO!**

BUT YOU DIDN'T EVEN HEAR THE QUESTION YET! I'M SORRY...

THAT'S FROM BEING AROUND THE KIDS ALL DAY

I SAY IT'S ONLY A TRICK TO MAKE US TURN BACK...

BUT JUST TO BE SAFE, LUCKY EDDIE, WHY DON'T YOU GO FIRST?

DANGER! QUICKSAND AHEAD

60

PRINTED IN BELGIUM BY
proost
INTERNATIONAL BOOK PRODUCTION